The Celestial Stoner

The Celestial Stoner

A Guide to the Zodiac

Matthew Petchinsky

Apophis Enterprises LLC

The Celestial Stoner: A Guide to the Zodiac
By: Matthew Petchinsky

Introduction: Astrology Meets Cannabis

Overview

Welcome to "The Celestial Stoner: A Guide to the Zodiac," a unique journey where astrology and cannabis intersect, offering you a personalized and spiritual approach to enhancing your cannabis experiences. In recent years, both astrology and cannabis have seen a resurgence in popularity, each providing comfort, insight, and a deeper connection to oneself and the universe. By combining the ancient wisdom of the zodiac with the therapeutic and recreational benefits of cannabis, this book aims to create a harmonious fusion that elevates both understanding and enjoyment.

Astrology, with its roots tracing back thousands of years, offers profound insights into our personalities, behaviors, and life paths based on the alignment of celestial bodies at the time of our birth. Each zodiac sign carries distinct traits, preferences, and challenges, shaping our unique identities. Meanwhile, cannabis, revered for its healing properties and ability to enhance sensory experiences, has been used for centuries across various cultures for medicinal, spiritual, and recreational purposes.

"The Celestial Stoner" bridges these two powerful realms, providing a comprehensive guide for integrating astrological insights into your cannabis journey. Whether you're a seasoned stoner or a curious newcomer, this book will help you navigate the stars and strains, fostering a deeper connection to both your astrological profile and your cannabis experience.

Purpose

The primary aim of "The Celestial Stoner" is to offer readers zodiac-based guidance for optimizing their cannabis use. By aligning your cannabis choices with your astrological profile, you can create more meaningful and personalized experiences that cater to your specific needs and preferences. This book is designed to:

1. **Enhance Self-Awareness**: By understanding how your zodiac sign influences your personality and behavior, you can make informed decisions about your cannabis use, aligning it with your natural tendencies and desires.

2. **Promote Holistic Well-being**: Combining astrology and cannabis encourages a holistic approach to wellness, integrating mind, body, and spirit. This synergy can help you achieve balance, relaxation, and a deeper connection to your inner self and the cosmos.

3. **Provide Practical Guidance**: Offering practical advice on cannabis strains, consumption methods, and lifestyle tips tailored to each zodiac sign, this book serves as a comprehensive resource for optimizing your cannabis experience.

4. **Foster a Sense of Community**: By exploring the intersection of astrology and cannabis, you join a growing community of individuals who appreciate the unique blend of cosmic wisdom and herbal healing, fostering connections and shared experiences.

Scope

"The Celestial Stoner" is structured to take you on an enlightening journey through the zodiac, exploring how each sign can uniquely benefit from and enhance their cannabis experience. The book is divided into several key sections:

1. **Introduction to Astrology and Cannabis**: An overview of the history and significance of astrology and cannabis, highlighting their individual benefits and the potential of their combination.

2. **Zodiac Profiles**: Detailed chapters dedicated to each of the twelve zodiac signs, providing:
   - **Astrological Insights**: An in-depth look at the characteristics, strengths, and challenges of each sign.

- ○ **Cannabis Strain Recommendations**: Suggested cannabis strains that complement the traits and preferences of each sign, enhancing their natural inclinations and providing tailored benefits.
- ○ **Consumption Tips**: Advice on the best consumption methods (e.g., smoking, vaping, edibles) for each sign, considering their personality and lifestyle.
- ○ **Lifestyle Advice**: Tips on how to incorporate cannabis into daily routines and rituals in a way that aligns with each sign's needs and tendencies.

3. **Astrological Events and Cannabis**: Guidance on how to navigate significant astrological events (e.g., retrogrades, eclipses) with the aid of cannabis, helping you maintain balance and well-being during cosmic shifts.

4. **Integration and Reflection**: Practical exercises and reflective prompts to help you integrate astrological insights and cannabis experiences into your daily life, fostering ongoing growth and self-awareness.

5. **Conclusion**: A summary of the key takeaways from the book, encouraging you to continue exploring the intersection of astrology and cannabis in your personal journey.

By the end of "The Celestial Stoner," you will have a comprehensive understanding of how to harmonize your astrological profile with your cannabis use, creating a personalized and enriching experience that enhances your connection to yourself and the universe. Welcome to a new dimension of self-discovery and cosmic cannabis enjoyment.

Chapter 1: Aries: The Pioneering Spirit
Zodiac Traits: The Dynamic and Assertive Nature of Aries
Aries, the first sign of the zodiac, is ruled by Mars, the planet of action, energy, and desire. Those born under this sign (March 21 - April 19) are known for their dynamic and assertive nature, embodying the pioneering spirit that drives them to be leaders and trailblazers in various aspects of life. Symbolized by the Ram, Aries individuals are characterized by their boldness, courage, and enthusiasm. They are natural-born leaders who thrive in environments that allow them to take initiative and pursue their goals with vigor and determination.

Key traits of Aries include:

1. **Energetic and Enthusiastic**: Aries are filled with boundless energy and enthusiasm, always ready to take on new challenges and adventures. They are often the life of the party, bringing excitement and vitality to any situation.
2. **Courageous and Bold**: Fearless in the face of adversity, Aries are known for their bravery and willingness to take risks. They are not afraid to stand up for what they believe in and will charge headfirst into new ventures.
3. **Independent and Self-reliant**: Aries value their independence and prefer to rely on themselves rather than others. They have a strong sense of self and are confident in their abilities to achieve their goals.
4. **Impulsive and Quick-tempered**: While their passion and drive are admirable, Aries can also be impulsive and quick-tempered. They may act on a whim without fully considering the consequences, leading to conflicts and misunderstandings.
5. **Competitive and Ambitious**: Aries have a competitive streak and thrive in situations where they can prove their prowess. They

are highly ambitious and constantly strive to be the best in whatever they do.

Cannabis Strains: Energizing and Stimulating for the Aries Adventurous Spirit

Given their energetic and adventurous nature, Aries benefit from cannabis strains that enhance their vitality and stimulate their active minds. The following strains are recommended to cater to Aries' dynamic personality:

1. **Green Crack**: This sativa-dominant strain is known for its invigorating effects, providing a sharp mental focus and an energetic boost. Green Crack is perfect for Aries who need a burst of energy to tackle their next adventure or creative project.
2. **Sour Diesel**: Another sativa-dominant strain, Sour Diesel offers uplifting and euphoric effects that enhance mood and promote mental clarity. Its stimulating properties make it an excellent choice for Aries who thrive on excitement and new experiences.
3. **Jack Herer**: A well-balanced hybrid, Jack Herer combines the uplifting effects of sativa with the relaxing properties of indica. This strain is ideal for Aries who need a balance of energy and relaxation, helping them stay focused and motivated while maintaining a sense of calm.
4. **Super Lemon Haze**: This zesty sativa-dominant strain delivers an energetic and creative high, perfect for Aries looking to boost their mood and productivity. Its refreshing citrus flavor adds an extra layer of enjoyment to the experience.
5. **Durban Poison**: Known for its potent and clear-headed effects, Durban Poison is a pure sativa that provides an intense burst of energy and mental stimulation. This strain is excellent for Aries who want to stay active and engaged throughout the day.

Consumption Settings: Social Settings and Activities for Aries' Outgoing Personality

Aries thrive in social settings and activities that allow them to showcase their outgoing and adventurous personality. When using cannabis, the following environments and activities are ideal for Aries:

1. **Outdoor Adventures**: Aries love the thrill of outdoor activities, whether it's hiking, biking, or exploring new trails. Consuming an energizing strain like Green Crack or Sour Diesel before heading out can enhance their experience, providing the stamina and mental clarity needed for their adventures.
2. **Social Gatherings**: Aries are natural social butterflies and enjoy being the center of attention at parties and gatherings. Strains like Jack Herer and Super Lemon Haze can help elevate their mood and keep them engaged in lively conversations and activities.
3. **Creative Pursuits**: Aries have a creative side that thrives on new ideas and projects. Engaging in artistic activities like painting, writing, or crafting while using a strain like Durban Poison can stimulate their imagination and drive their creative endeavors.
4. **Fitness and Exercise**: Physical activity is essential for Aries to channel their abundant energy. Consuming a strain like Sour Diesel before a workout or fitness class can boost their motivation and enhance their performance.
5. **Competitive Games**: Aries' competitive nature makes them enjoy games and sports where they can test their skills. Participating in activities like team sports, video games, or board games with friends while using a stimulating strain can heighten their enjoyment and keep them focused.

By understanding the unique traits and preferences of Aries, "The Celestial Stoner" provides tailored cannabis recommendations and consumption settings that align with their dynamic and assertive nature. This personalized approach ensures that Aries can fully embrace their adventurous spirit while enjoying the benefits of cannabis, creating an experience that is both fulfilling and empowering.

Check out my Virtual dispensary for all your hemp needs: https://shift.store/sg1fan23477/retail

Chapter 2: Taurus: The Sensual Connoisseur

Zodiac Traits: Exploring Taurus' Love for Comfort and Sensory Pleasures

Taurus, the second sign of the zodiac, is ruled by Venus, the planet of love, beauty, and pleasure. Those born under this sign (April 20 - May 20) are known for their deep appreciation of comfort, stability, and the finer things in life. Represented by the Bull, Taurus individuals are grounded, reliable, and possess a strong connection to the physical world. They find joy in indulging their senses, whether through delicious food, beautiful art, soothing music, or luxurious surroundings.

Key traits of Taurus include:

1. **Loyal and Dependable**: Taurus individuals are known for their steadfast loyalty and reliability. They are the friends and partners you can always count on, providing unwavering support and stability.

2. **Patient and Persistent**: Taurus is characterized by patience and a determined nature. They are willing to put in the time and effort to achieve their goals, often working methodically and persistently until they succeed.

3. **Appreciation for Beauty and Comfort**: Ruled by Venus, Taurus has a natural affinity for beauty and comfort. They seek out and create environments that are aesthetically pleasing and comfortable, reveling in sensory pleasures.

4. **Stubborn and Resistant to Change**: While their determination is admirable, Taurus can also be quite stubborn and resistant to change. They prefer routine and familiarity, often sticking to what they know and love.

5. **Practical and Grounded**: Taurus individuals are practical and grounded, with a strong connection to the physical and material world. They have a keen sense of what is necessary and valuable, often excelling in managing resources and finances.

Cannabis Strains: Enhancing Sensory Experiences and Relaxation for Taurus

Given their love for comfort and sensory pleasures, Taurus benefits from cannabis strains that enhance relaxation and heighten their sensory experiences. The following strains are recommended to cater to Taurus' luxurious tastes:

1. **Blue Dream**: This well-balanced hybrid strain offers a gentle, relaxing high that enhances sensory perception without overwhelming the user. Blue Dream is perfect for Taurus who want to unwind and enjoy the finer things in life with a clear mind.
2. **Granddaddy Purple**: Known for its deep relaxation and soothing effects, Granddaddy Purple is an indica-dominant strain that melts away stress and tension. Its rich, grape-like flavor adds to the sensory indulgence, making it ideal for a cozy night in.
3. **Bubba Kush**: This indica strain is renowned for its heavy body high and calming effects. Bubba Kush is perfect for Taurus who want to sink into a state of blissful relaxation, enjoying the comforting embrace of this potent strain.
4. **Northern Lights**: Another indica-dominant strain, Northern Lights provides a deeply relaxing and tranquil experience. Its earthy, sweet aroma and flavor enhance the sensory pleasure, making it a favorite for Taurus seeking peace and comfort.
5. **Strawberry Cough**: For a more uplifting experience, Strawberry Cough offers a sativa-dominant high that stimulates the senses while maintaining a sense of calm. Its sweet, fruity flavor and aroma are sure to delight Taurus' taste buds.

Consumption Settings: Indulgent, Relaxing Environments for Taurus' Luxurious Tastes

Taurus thrives in environments that cater to their love for luxury, comfort, and sensory pleasures. When using cannabis, the following settings and activities are ideal for Taurus:

1. **Home Spa Day**: Transform your home into a spa-like retreat, complete with scented candles, soothing music, and plush robes. Enjoy a relaxing soak in the bath with a strain like Granddaddy Purple or Bubba Kush to enhance the sense of tranquility and indulgence.

2. **Gourmet Dining Experience**: Taurus' love for good food makes a gourmet dining experience an excellent setting for cannabis consumption. Pair a strain like Blue Dream with a home-cooked meal or a tasting menu at a fine dining restaurant to elevate the sensory pleasure of each bite.

3. **Nature Retreat**: Escape to nature for a peaceful retreat, whether it's a cabin in the woods, a beachside bungalow, or a scenic camping spot. Enjoy the calming effects of Northern Lights while taking in the beauty of the natural surroundings.

4. **Art and Music Appreciation**: Taurus has a deep appreciation for art and music. Visit an art gallery, attend a live concert, or create your own art at home while using a strain like Strawberry Cough to heighten your sensory experience and creative expression.

5. **Luxurious Movie Night**: Create a cozy and luxurious movie-watching environment at home with soft blankets, comfortable seating, and your favorite snacks. Enjoy a relaxing strain like Bubba Kush while watching a film that appeals to your aesthetic and emotional sensibilities.

By understanding the unique traits and preferences of Taurus, "The Celestial Stoner" provides tailored cannabis recommendations and consumption settings that align with their love for comfort, beauty, and sensory pleasures. This personalized approach ensures that Taurus can fully embrace their luxurious tastes while enjoying the benefits of cannabis, creating an experience that is both indulgent and deeply satisfying.

Check out my Virtual dispensary for all your hemp needs: https://shift.store/sg1fan23477/retail

Chapter 3: Gemini: The Social Butterfly

Zodiac Traits: Describing Gemini's Communicative and Sociable Nature

Gemini, the third sign of the zodiac, is ruled by Mercury, the planet of communication, intellect, and travel. Those born under this sign (May 21 - June 20) are known for their quick wit, curiosity, and adaptability. Represented by the Twins, Gemini individuals have a dual nature that allows them to see multiple perspectives and adapt to different social situations with ease. They are natural communicators and thrive in environments where they can engage in lively conversations and exchange ideas.

Key traits of Gemini include:

1. **Curious and Intellectual**: Gemini are intellectually driven and possess an insatiable curiosity. They love learning new things, exploring diverse topics, and engaging in stimulating discussions.
2. **Sociable and Outgoing**: Geminis are social butterflies who enjoy meeting new people and forming connections. They thrive in social settings and are often the life of the party, charming others with their wit and humor.
3. **Adaptable and Flexible**: Gemini's dual nature makes them highly adaptable and flexible. They can easily switch between different roles and environments, making them versatile and resourceful in various situations.
4. **Communicative and Expressive**: Ruled by Mercury, Gemini excels in communication. They are articulate, expressive, and skilled at conveying their thoughts and ideas clearly and persuasively.
5. **Restless and Impulsive**: While their curiosity and adaptability are strengths, Gemini can also be restless and impulsive. They

may struggle with staying focused on one task for long periods and may quickly lose interest if not constantly stimulated.

Cannabis Strains: Promoting Sociability and Mental Stimulation for Gemini

Given their sociable and intellectually driven nature, Gemini benefits from cannabis strains that enhance mental stimulation and promote sociability. The following strains are recommended to cater to Gemini's dynamic personality:

1. **Super Silver Haze**: This sativa-dominant strain is known for its energizing and uplifting effects. Super Silver Haze enhances mental clarity and creativity, making it perfect for Gemini who want to engage in lively conversations and intellectual pursuits.
2. **Pineapple Express**: A well-balanced hybrid, Pineapple Express provides a gentle cerebral high that promotes happiness and sociability. Its sweet and fruity flavor adds to the enjoyment, making it an excellent choice for social gatherings.
3. **Lemon Haze**: Known for its uplifting and euphoric effects, Lemon Haze is a sativa strain that stimulates the mind and enhances focus. This strain is ideal for Gemini who want to stay mentally sharp and engaged in dynamic environments.
4. **Jack Herer**: This sativa-dominant hybrid offers a balanced high that promotes mental stimulation and relaxation. Jack Herer is perfect for Gemini who need a strain that keeps them alert and communicative while providing a sense of calm.
5. **Chocolope**: Chocolope is a sativa strain that delivers an energizing and motivational high. Its sweet and chocolatey flavor is a delight, and its effects are perfect for Gemini looking to stay active and socially engaged.

Consumption Settings: Dynamic and Varied Social Gatherings for Gemini

Gemini thrives in dynamic and varied social settings that keep them engaged and stimulated. When using cannabis, the following environments and activities are ideal for Gemini:

1. **Networking Events**: Gemini's love for meeting new people and exchanging ideas makes networking events a perfect setting for cannabis consumption. Enjoy a strain like Super Silver Haze to enhance your mental clarity and confidence while engaging with others.

2. **Trivia Nights**: Engaging in trivia nights at local bars or with friends at home can be a fun and intellectually stimulating activity for Gemini. A strain like Lemon Haze can help keep your mind sharp and focused during the game.

3. **Book Clubs and Discussion Groups**: Participating in book clubs or discussion groups allows Gemini to indulge their intellectual curiosity and enjoy stimulating conversations. A strain like Jack Herer can enhance your ability to articulate your thoughts and ideas.

4. **Travel and Exploration**: Gemini's adventurous spirit thrives on travel and exploration. Whether it's a weekend getaway or a spontaneous road trip, a strain like Pineapple Express can enhance the experience, keeping you energized and sociable.

5. **Art and Culture Events**: Visiting art galleries, attending theater performances, or exploring cultural festivals are excellent activities for Gemini. A strain like Chocolope can heighten your senses and keep you engaged in the vibrant atmosphere.

By understanding the unique traits and preferences of Gemini, "The Celestial Stoner" provides tailored cannabis recommendations and consumption settings that align with their communicative and sociable nature. This personalized approach ensures that Gemini can fully embrace their dynamic personality while enjoying the benefits of cannabis, creating an experience that is both intellectually stimulating and socially fulfilling.

Check out my Virtual dispensary for all your hemp needs: https://shift.store/sg1fan23477/retail

Chapter 4: Cancer: The Comfort Seeker
Zodiac Traits: Examining Cancer's Need for Emotional Security and Comfort

Cancer, the fourth sign of the zodiac, is ruled by the Moon, which governs emotions, intuition, and the subconscious mind. Those born under this sign (June 21 - July 22) are deeply sensitive and nurturing individuals who value emotional security and comfort above all else. Represented by the Crab, Cancer individuals possess a hard exterior that protects their soft, vulnerable inner world. They are known for their loyalty, empathy, and strong connection to family and home.

Key traits of Cancer include:

1. **Emotional and Intuitive**: Cancer individuals are highly in tune with their emotions and the emotions of others. Their intuition is strong, allowing them to sense and respond to the needs and feelings of those around them.

2. **Nurturing and Caring**: Cancer is the caregiver of the zodiac, always willing to offer support, comfort, and protection to loved ones. They find fulfillment in nurturing others and creating a safe, loving environment.

3. **Home-Oriented and Protective**: Home is where Cancer feels most secure. They take great pride in creating a cozy, inviting space and are fiercely protective of their family and close friends.

4. **Loyal and Devoted**: Once Cancer forms a bond, they are incredibly loyal and devoted. They value deep, meaningful relationships and will go to great lengths to maintain and protect them.

5. **Sensitive and Moody**: While their sensitivity is a strength, it can also make Cancer prone to mood swings and emotional

vulnerability. They may retreat into their shell when feeling overwhelmed or hurt.

Cannabis Strains: Providing Calming Effects and Stress Relief for Cancer

Given their need for emotional security and comfort, Cancer benefits from cannabis strains that offer calming effects and stress relief. The following strains are recommended to cater to Cancer's nurturing and sensitive nature:

1. **Harlequin**: This sativa-dominant strain is high in CBD, providing gentle relaxation without strong psychoactive effects. Harlequin is perfect for Cancer who seek stress relief and a sense of calm while remaining clear-headed.
2. **ACDC**: Another high-CBD strain, ACDC offers soothing effects that alleviate anxiety and stress without causing a significant high. This strain is ideal for Cancer who want to relax and unwind while maintaining emotional balance.
3. **Blueberry**: Known for its calming and euphoric effects, Blueberry is an indica-dominant strain that melts away stress and tension. Its sweet, berry flavor adds to the comforting experience, making it perfect for a cozy night in.
4. **Northern Lights**: This classic indica strain provides deep relaxation and tranquility, helping to ease anxiety and promote restful sleep. Northern Lights is ideal for Cancer who need to retreat and recharge in a safe, nurturing environment.
5. **Granddaddy Purple**: With its potent relaxing effects and soothing properties, Granddaddy Purple is an excellent choice for Cancer seeking to alleviate stress and find emotional comfort. Its rich, grape-like flavor adds to the overall sense of indulgence and relaxation.

Consumption Settings: Cozy, Intimate Settings for Cancer's Need for Safety and Nurturing

Cancer thrives in cozy, intimate settings that provide a sense of safety and nurturing. When using cannabis, the following environments and activities are ideal for Cancer:

1. **Home Sanctuary**: Transform your home into a sanctuary of comfort and security. Create a cozy space with soft blankets, pillows, and warm lighting. Enjoy a strain like Blueberry or Granddaddy Purple while relaxing with a good book or watching a favorite movie.

2. **Bath Time Bliss**: Indulge in a soothing bath with calming essential oils, candles, and relaxing music. Use a strain like Northern Lights or ACDC to enhance the sense of tranquility and help you unwind after a long day.

3. **Family Gatherings**: Spend quality time with family and close friends in a comfortable, familiar environment. Share a strain like Harlequin that promotes relaxation and sociability, fostering deep connections and meaningful conversations.

4. **Meditation and Mindfulness**: Practice meditation or mindfulness exercises in a quiet, peaceful setting. Use a strain like ACDC or Harlequin to help calm your mind and enhance your sense of inner peace and emotional balance.

5. **Cooking and Baking**: Engage in the comforting and creative activity of cooking or baking at home. Choose a strain like Blueberry to enjoy the process and enhance your sensory experience as you prepare and savor delicious meals.

By understanding the unique traits and preferences of Cancer, "The Celestial Stoner" provides tailored cannabis recommendations and consumption settings that align with their need for emotional security and comfort. This personalized approach ensures that Cancer can fully embrace their nurturing and sensitive nature while enjoying the benefits of cannabis, creating an experience that is both soothing and emotionally fulfilling.

Check out my Virtual dispensary for all your hemp needs: https://shift.store/sg1fan23477/retail

Chapter 5: Leo: The Radiant Star
Zodiac Traits: Discussing Leo's Charismatic and Theatrical Nature

Leo, the fifth sign of the zodiac, is ruled by the Sun, the center of our solar system, symbolizing vitality, authority, and self-expression. Those born under this sign (July 23 - August 22) are known for their charismatic, confident, and theatrical nature. Represented by the Lion, Leo individuals possess a regal presence and a natural inclination to be in the spotlight. They are warm-hearted, generous, and love to express themselves creatively, often captivating those around them with their charm and enthusiasm.

Key traits of Leo include:

1. **Charismatic and Confident**: Leos exude confidence and charisma, effortlessly drawing attention and admiration. They have a magnetic personality that makes them natural leaders and performers.

2. **Creative and Expressive**: Creativity flows naturally for Leos, who thrive on expressing themselves through various forms of art, drama, and performance. Their dramatic flair often leads them to pursue activities where they can showcase their talents.

3. **Generous and Warm-hearted**: Leos are known for their generosity and warmth. They love to make others feel special and appreciated, often going out of their way to create joyful experiences for their loved ones.

4. **Ambitious and Determined**: Driven by a desire for recognition and success, Leos are highly ambitious and determined. They set high goals for themselves and pursue them with passion and dedication.

5. **Proud and Stubborn**: While their pride is a source of strength, it can also make Leos stubborn and resistant to criticism. They have a strong sense of self-worth and may struggle to accept feedback that challenges their self-image.

Cannabis Strains: Energizing and Enhancing Creativity for Leo's Dramatic Flair

Given their charismatic and creative nature, Leo benefits from cannabis strains that energize and enhance creativity. The following strains are recommended to cater to Leo's dynamic personality:

1. **Sour Diesel**: This sativa-dominant strain is known for its energizing and uplifting effects. Sour Diesel enhances creativity and mental clarity, making it perfect for Leos who want to engage in artistic pursuits or social gatherings.
2. **Tangie**: With its refreshing citrus flavor and stimulating effects, Tangie is a sativa strain that promotes creativity and euphoria. It's ideal for Leos looking to boost their mood and express their artistic talents.
3. **Green Crack**: Known for its invigorating and focused high, Green Crack is a sativa-dominant strain that provides a burst of energy and creativity. It's perfect for Leos who need an extra push to tackle creative projects or take center stage.
4. **Blue Dream**: This well-balanced hybrid strain offers a gentle, uplifting high that enhances creativity and relaxation. Blue Dream is perfect for Leos who want to enjoy a creative flow without feeling too overwhelmed.
5. **Pineapple Express**: A hybrid strain known for its balanced effects, Pineapple Express provides an energizing and euphoric high that enhances creativity and sociability. It's a great choice for Leos who want to shine at social gatherings.

Consumption Settings: Proposing Settings that Allow Leo to Shine and Perform

Leos thrive in settings that allow them to shine and perform, showcasing their charismatic and theatrical nature. When using cannabis, the following environments and activities are ideal for Leo:

1. **Artistic Gatherings**: Leos love to express their creativity in social settings. Hosting or attending an art show, open mic night, or creative workshop allows them to showcase their talents while enjoying the stimulating effects of strains like Tangie or Green Crack.

2. **Themed Parties**: Leos enjoy being the life of the party. Hosting a themed party where guests can dress up and engage in fun activities is a perfect setting for Leos to shine. A strain like Pineapple Express can enhance their sociability and ensure they stay energized throughout the event.

3. **Theater and Performances**: Whether participating in or watching a theater performance, Leos thrive in environments where they can indulge their love for drama and expression. Consuming a strain like Sour Diesel beforehand can boost their confidence and creativity, enhancing their experience.

4. **Creative Projects**: Engaging in creative projects such as painting, writing, or crafting allows Leos to channel their artistic energy. A strain like Blue Dream can help them maintain a steady flow of creativity and focus while working on their masterpiece.

5. **Social Media and Content Creation**: Leos love to be seen and heard, making social media and content creation ideal platforms for their self-expression. Using a strain like Green Crack can provide the energy and inspiration needed to produce engaging content and connect with their audience.

By understanding the unique traits and preferences of Leo, "The Celestial Stoner" provides tailored cannabis recommendations and consumption settings that align with their charismatic and theatrical nature. This personalized approach ensures that Leos can fully embrace their dynamic personality while enjoying the benefits of cannabis, creating an experience that is both energizing and creatively fulfilling.

Check out my Virtual dispensary for all your hemp needs: https://shift.store/sg1fan23477/retail

Chapter 6: Virgo: The Methodical Analyst
Zodiac Traits: Delving into Virgo's Detail-Oriented and Meticulous Nature

Virgo, the sixth sign of the zodiac, is ruled by Mercury, the planet of communication, intellect, and analysis. Those born under this sign (August 23 - September 22) are known for their keen attention to detail, analytical thinking, and meticulous nature. Represented by the Virgin, Virgo individuals strive for perfection and often set high standards for themselves and others. They are practical, reliable, and deeply committed to their responsibilities, making them invaluable in both personal and professional settings.

Key traits of Virgo include:

1. **Detail-Oriented and Meticulous**: Virgos have a natural ability to notice and analyze even the smallest details. They excel in tasks that require precision and accuracy, often taking a methodical approach to their work.
2. **Analytical and Logical**: Virgos are highly analytical and possess strong problem-solving skills. They rely on logic and reason to make decisions and are adept at breaking down complex issues into manageable parts.
3. **Practical and Reliable**: Known for their practicality and reliability, Virgos are often the go-to person for advice and support. They have a strong sense of duty and are committed to fulfilling their responsibilities.
4. **Health-Conscious and Hygienic**: Virgos place a high value on health and hygiene. They are often mindful of their diet, exercise, and overall well-being, striving to maintain a balanced and healthy lifestyle.

5. **Reserved and Modest**: While Virgos are highly capable and intelligent, they tend to be reserved and modest about their achievements. They prefer to work behind the scenes rather than seek the spotlight.

Cannabis Strains: Aiding Focus and Mental Clarity for Virgo's Methodical Mind

Given their detail-oriented and meticulous nature, Virgo benefits from cannabis strains that aid focus and mental clarity. The following strains are recommended to cater to Virgo's analytical and methodical personality:

1. **Harlequin**: This sativa-dominant strain is high in CBD, providing clear-headed effects and enhancing focus without significant psychoactive impact. Harlequin is perfect for Virgos who want to maintain mental clarity while reducing stress and anxiety.
2. **Cinex**: Known for its uplifting and focusing effects, Cinex is a sativa strain that enhances creativity and mental clarity. It's ideal for Virgos who need to stay sharp and engaged in detailed tasks or analytical work.
3. **Green Crack**: This sativa-dominant strain offers an invigorating and focused high, providing a burst of energy and mental clarity. Green Crack is perfect for Virgos who need an extra boost to tackle complex projects or stay productive throughout the day.
4. **ACDC**: Another high-CBD strain, ACDC provides calming effects without significant psychoactive impact. It helps reduce anxiety and stress, allowing Virgos to stay focused and clear-headed while working on detailed tasks.
5. **Super Lemon Haze**: Known for its uplifting and energizing effects, Super Lemon Haze is a sativa-dominant strain that enhances focus and creativity. It's perfect for Virgos who want to maintain a positive and productive mindset while engaging in their hobbies or work.

Consumption Settings: Serene Environments for Virgo's Detailed Tasks and Hobbies

Virgo thrives in serene environments that allow them to focus on detailed tasks or hobbies without distraction. When using cannabis, the following settings and activities are ideal for Virgo:

1. **Home Office or Study Space**: Create a dedicated home office or study space that is organized, clean, and free from distractions. Use a strain like Harlequin or Cinex to enhance focus and productivity while working on detailed tasks or analytical projects.
2. **Gardening and Plant Care**: Virgos often find joy in gardening and caring for plants, activities that require attention to detail and patience. Enjoy a strain like ACDC or Super Lemon Haze to stay calm and focused while tending to your garden.
3. **Art and Craft Projects**: Engaging in art and craft projects allows Virgos to express their creativity while paying attention to intricate details. Use a strain like Green Crack to maintain mental clarity and energy while working on your creative endeavors.
4. **Cooking and Baking**: Virgos' meticulous nature makes them excellent cooks and bakers. Enjoy a strain like Super Lemon Haze to enhance your focus and creativity while experimenting with new recipes or perfecting your culinary skills.
5. **Yoga and Meditation**: Practicing yoga and meditation helps Virgos maintain a balanced and healthy lifestyle. Use a strain like ACDC to promote relaxation and mental clarity, allowing you to stay present and focused during your practice.

By understanding the unique traits and preferences of Virgo, "The Celestial Stoner" provides tailored cannabis recommendations and consumption settings that align with their detail-oriented and methodical nature. This personalized approach ensures that Virgos can fully embrace their analytical and meticulous personality while enjoying the benefits of cannabis, creating an experience that is both focused and fulfilling.

Check out my Virtual dispensary for all your hemp needs: https://shift.store/sg1fan23477/retail

Chapter 7: Libra: The Harmonious Partner

Zodiac Traits: Exploring Libra's Love for Balance and Relationships

Libra, the seventh sign of the zodiac, is ruled by Venus, the planet of love, beauty, and harmony. Those born under this sign (September 23 - October 22) are known for their strong sense of balance, justice, and deep appreciation for relationships. Represented by the Scales, Libra individuals seek harmony in all aspects of their lives and are often seen as the mediators and peacemakers of the zodiac. They are charming, diplomatic, and have a natural ability to see multiple perspectives, making them adept at navigating social situations and fostering positive relationships.

Key traits of Libra include:

1. **Balanced and Harmonious**: Libras strive for balance and harmony in their lives. They are drawn to beauty and symmetry, often seeking to create peaceful and aesthetically pleasing environments.

2. **Diplomatic and Fair**: Libra individuals are natural diplomats who value fairness and justice. They are skilled at resolving conflicts and finding compromises that satisfy all parties involved.

3. **Social and Charming**: Libras are social butterflies who enjoy being around others. They have a natural charm and grace that makes them likable and easy to get along with.

4. **Indecisive and People-Pleasing**: While their desire for harmony is a strength, it can also make Libras indecisive and overly concerned with pleasing others. They may struggle to make decisions

when faced with multiple options and may prioritize others'
needs over their own.

5. **Appreciative of Beauty and Art**: Ruled by Venus, Libras have
   a deep appreciation for beauty, art, and culture. They are drawn
   to artistic expressions and often have a keen eye for design and
   aesthetics.

Cannabis Strains: Promoting Social Harmony and Enhancing Interpersonal Connections for Libra

Given their love for balance and relationships, Libra benefits from
cannabis strains that promote social harmony and enhance interper-
sonal connections. The following strains are recommended to cater to
Libra's diplomatic and sociable personality:

1. **Blue Dream**: This well-balanced hybrid strain offers a gentle, uplifting high that promotes relaxation and sociability. Blue Dream
   is perfect for Libras who want to enjoy harmonious social interactions and enhance their creative pursuits.
2. **Strawberry Cough**: Known for its sweet, fruity flavor and uplifting effects, Strawberry Cough is a sativa strain that enhances
   mood and sociability. It's ideal for Libras who want to engage in
   lively conversations and social gatherings.
3. **Pineapple Express**: A hybrid strain known for its balanced effects, Pineapple Express provides an energizing and euphoric high
   that promotes creativity and social interaction. It's a great choice
   for Libras who want to shine in social settings.
4. **Harlequin**: This sativa-dominant strain is high in CBD, providing clear-headed effects and enhancing focus without significant
   psychoactive impact. Harlequin is perfect for Libras who want to
   stay calm and balanced while engaging in social activities.
5. **ACDC**: Another high-CBD strain, ACDC offers soothing effects
   that alleviate anxiety and stress without causing a significant high.

This strain is ideal for Libras who seek to maintain harmony and emotional balance in their interactions.

Consumption Settings: Social Activities Involving Partnerships or Groups for Libra's Diplomatic Skills

Libra thrives in social settings that involve partnerships or groups, allowing them to utilize their diplomatic skills and foster positive connections. When using cannabis, the following environments and activities are ideal for Libra:

1. **Dinner Parties**: Hosting or attending dinner parties allows Libras to enjoy good food, beautiful settings, and engaging conversations. Use a strain like Blue Dream or Pineapple Express to enhance the sociable and harmonious atmosphere.

2. **Group Art Projects**: Participating in group art projects or collaborative creative activities allows Libras to express their appreciation for beauty and art while working with others. A strain like Strawberry Cough can boost creativity and sociability, making the experience more enjoyable.

3. **Book Clubs**: Joining a book club provides Libras with the opportunity to engage in thoughtful discussions and connect with others over shared interests. Use a strain like Harlequin to stay focused and articulate during discussions.

4. **Yoga Classes**: Attending group yoga classes helps Libras maintain physical and mental balance while connecting with like-minded individuals. A strain like ACDC can enhance relaxation and focus, making the practice more fulfilling.

5. **Outdoor Picnics**: Enjoying a picnic in a beautiful outdoor setting with friends or family allows Libras to combine their love for nature, beauty, and social interaction. A strain like Blue Dream can enhance the overall sense of harmony and enjoyment.

By understanding the unique traits and preferences of Libra, "The Celestial Stoner" provides tailored cannabis recommendations and consumption settings that align with their love for balance and relationships. This personalized approach ensures that Libras can fully embrace their diplomatic and sociable nature while enjoying the benefits of cannabis, creating an experience that is both harmonious and socially fulfilling.

Check out my Virtual dispensary for all your hemp needs: https://shift.store/sg1fan23477/retail

Chapter 8: Scorpio: The Intense Investigator

Zodiac Traits: Discussing Scorpio's Intense and Passionate Nature

Scorpio, the eighth sign of the zodiac, is ruled by Pluto, the planet of transformation, and Mars, the planet of action and desire. Those born under this sign (October 23 - November 21) are known for their intense, passionate, and mysterious nature. Represented by the Scorpion, Scorpio individuals are deeply emotional and possess a magnetic presence that draws others to them. They are known for their determination, resourcefulness, and ability to delve into the depths of any situation, making them natural investigators and truth-seekers.

Key traits of Scorpio include:

1. **Intense and Passionate**: Scorpios feel emotions deeply and passionately. They approach life with intensity, whether it's in their relationships, work, or personal interests.

2. **Mysterious and Magnetic**: There is an enigmatic quality to Scorpios that makes them intriguing and magnetic. They often keep their true thoughts and feelings hidden, revealing them only to those they trust deeply.

3. **Determined and Resilient**: Once Scorpios set their sights on a goal, they pursue it with unwavering determination and resilience. They are not easily deterred and can overcome significant obstacles to achieve their aims.

4. **Resourceful and Insightful**: Scorpios possess a keen insight and resourcefulness that allows them to navigate complex situations effectively. They are adept at uncovering hidden truths and understanding the deeper aspects of human nature.

5. **Loyal and Protective**: Scorpios are fiercely loyal and protective of their loved ones. They form deep bonds and are willing to go to great lengths to support and defend those they care about.

Cannabis Strains: Deep, Potent Strains for Scorpio's Desire for Profound Experiences

Given their intense and passionate nature, Scorpio benefits from deep, potent cannabis strains that match their desire for profound and transformative experiences. The following strains are recommended to cater to Scorpio's intense personality:

1. **Northern Lights**: This classic indica strain provides a deeply relaxing and tranquil experience, helping Scorpios to unwind and explore their inner thoughts. Its potent effects are ideal for those seeking a profound and restful experience.
2. **Granddaddy Purple**: Known for its heavy relaxation and calming properties, Granddaddy Purple is an indica-dominant strain that helps Scorpios delve into deep emotional and psychological states. Its rich flavor and powerful effects make it perfect for introspective sessions.
3. **Girl Scout Cookies (GSC)**: This hybrid strain offers a balanced mix of euphoria and relaxation, making it suitable for Scorpios who want to explore their emotions while maintaining mental clarity. GSC's potent effects are perfect for deep, transformative experiences.
4. **OG Kush**: Known for its strong and long-lasting effects, OG Kush is a hybrid strain that provides a powerful body high and mental clarity. It's ideal for Scorpios seeking to explore deeper psychological states and uncover hidden truths.
5. **White Widow**: This balanced hybrid strain offers a blend of euphoria and relaxation, making it suitable for Scorpios who want to engage in deep conversations and emotional exploration.

Its potent effects help in achieving a profound and transformative experience.

Consumption Settings: Transformative Settings for Scorpio's Deep Emotional and Psychological Exploration

Scorpio thrives in transformative settings that allow them to explore deeper emotional and psychological states. When using cannabis, the following environments and activities are ideal for Scorpio:

1. **Meditation and Introspection**: Create a serene and quiet space for meditation and introspection. Use a strain like Northern Lights or Granddaddy Purple to enhance your ability to relax deeply and explore your inner thoughts and emotions.

2. **Deep Conversations**: Engage in deep, meaningful conversations with trusted friends or partners. A strain like Girl Scout Cookies (GSC) or White Widow can help facilitate open and honest dialogue, allowing Scorpios to connect on a profound level.

3. **Journaling and Creative Writing**: Set aside time for journaling or creative writing to explore your thoughts and emotions. Use a strain like OG Kush to enhance your focus and introspective abilities, allowing you to uncover hidden truths and insights.

4. **Artistic Expression**: Engage in artistic activities such as painting, sculpting, or music to channel your intense emotions and creativity. A strain like White Widow can help enhance your artistic expression and provide a deeper connection to your creative process.

5. **Nature Retreats**: Spend time in nature to reconnect with your inner self and the natural world. Whether it's a solitary hike or a secluded cabin retreat, a strain like Northern Lights can help you achieve a sense of peace and transformation in a natural setting.

By understanding the unique traits and preferences of Scorpio, "The Celestial Stoner" provides tailored cannabis recommendations and consumption settings that align with their intense and passionate nature. This personalized approach ensures that Scorpios can fully embrace their desire for profound experiences while enjoying the benefits of cannabis, creating an experience that is both transformative and deeply fulfilling.

Check out my Virtual dispensary for all your hemp needs: https://shift.store/sg1fan23477/retail

Chapter 9: Sagittarius: The Adventurous Philosopher
Zodiac Traits: Covering Sagittarius' Quest for Knowledge and Exploration

Sagittarius, the ninth sign of the zodiac, is ruled by Jupiter, the planet of expansion, growth, and wisdom. Those born under this sign (November 22 - December 21) are known for their adventurous spirit, love of freedom, and insatiable quest for knowledge. Represented by the Archer, Sagittarius individuals are explorers and philosophers at heart, always seeking to broaden their horizons and understand the world around them. They are optimistic, enthusiastic, and have a deep love for travel and learning.

Key traits of Sagittarius include:

1. **Adventurous and Free-Spirited**: Sagittarians have a strong desire for adventure and freedom. They are always ready to explore new places, meet new people, and try new experiences.
2. **Philosophical and Inquisitive**: Sagittarius individuals have a natural curiosity and a love for knowledge. They enjoy pondering the big questions in life and are drawn to philosophy, religion, and higher education.
3. **Optimistic and Enthusiastic**: Sagittarians are known for their optimism and enthusiasm. They have a positive outlook on life and are always looking for the silver lining in any situation.
4. **Honest and Direct**: Sagittarius individuals value honesty and are known for their direct communication style. They appreciate straightforwardness and are not afraid to speak their minds.

5. **Independent and Restless**: While their independence is a strength, it can also make Sagittarians restless and impatient. They dislike being tied down and may struggle with commitments and routine.

Cannabis Strains: Stimulating the Mind and Enhancing Philosophical Pondering for Sagittarius

Given their quest for knowledge and exploration, Sagittarius benefits from cannabis strains that stimulate the mind and enhance philosophical pondering. The following strains are recommended to cater to Sagittarius' adventurous and inquisitive nature:

1. **Jack Herer**: This sativa-dominant strain is known for its stimulating and clear-headed effects. Jack Herer enhances creativity and mental clarity, making it perfect for Sagittarians who want to engage in philosophical discussions or deep thinking.
2. **Sour Diesel**: Known for its energizing and uplifting effects, Sour Diesel is a sativa strain that promotes mental stimulation and focus. It's ideal for Sagittarians who want to stay active and engaged while exploring new ideas and experiences.
3. **Super Silver Haze**: This sativa-dominant strain offers a balanced high that stimulates the mind and provides a sense of euphoria. Super Silver Haze is perfect for Sagittarians who want to enhance their philosophical pondering and creativity.
4. **Pineapple Express**: A well-balanced hybrid, Pineapple Express provides an energizing and euphoric high that promotes creativity and mental clarity. It's a great choice for Sagittarians who want to stay active and inspired while exploring new places.
5. **Green Crack**: Known for its invigorating and focused high, Green Crack is a sativa-dominant strain that provides a burst of energy and mental clarity. It's perfect for Sagittarians who need an extra push to stay productive and engaged in their adventures.

Consumption Settings: Outdoor or Travel-Related Settings for Sagittarius to Explore and Learn

Sagittarius thrives in outdoor or travel-related settings that allow them to explore and learn. When using cannabis, the following environments and activities are ideal for Sagittarius:

1. **Hiking and Nature Trails**: Sagittarians love being in nature and exploring the great outdoors. Use a strain like Sour Diesel or Green Crack to stay energized and focused while hiking through scenic trails and discovering new landscapes.

2. **Cultural Festivals and Events**: Attending cultural festivals and events allows Sagittarians to immerse themselves in new experiences and learn about different cultures. A strain like Pineapple Express can enhance the overall sense of excitement and curiosity.

3. **Travel and Exploration**: Whether it's a road trip, backpacking adventure, or international travel, Sagittarians thrive on exploring new places. Use a strain like Jack Herer or Super Silver Haze to stay mentally sharp and inspired during your travels.

4. **Outdoor Meditation and Yoga**: Practicing meditation or yoga in an outdoor setting can help Sagittarians connect with their inner selves and the natural world. A strain like Super Silver Haze can enhance the sense of tranquility and mindfulness.

5. **Philosophical Discussions and Book Clubs**: Engaging in philosophical discussions or joining a book club allows Sagittarians to share their ideas and learn from others. A strain like Jack Herer can help stimulate deep thinking and enhance your ability to articulate your thoughts.

By understanding the unique traits and preferences of Sagittarius, "The Celestial Stoner" provides tailored cannabis recommendations and consumption settings that align with their adventurous and philosophical nature. This personalized approach ensures that Sagittarians can fully embrace their love for exploration and knowledge while enjoying the benefits of cannabis, creating an experience that is both intellectually stimulating and deeply fulfilling.

Check out my Virtual dispensary for all your hemp needs: https://shift.store/sg1fan23477/retail

Chapter 10: Capricorn: The Ambitious Climber
Zodiac Traits: Analyzing Capricorn's Disciplined and Ambitious Nature

Capricorn, the tenth sign of the zodiac, is ruled by Saturn, the planet of discipline, responsibility, and structure. Those born under this sign (December 22 - January 19) are known for their disciplined, ambitious, and hardworking nature. Represented by the Goat, Capricorn individuals are determined to climb to the top of their chosen fields and achieve their goals. They are practical, responsible, and have a strong sense of duty, making them reliable and dependable in both personal and professional settings.

Key traits of Capricorn include:

1. **Disciplined and Hardworking**: Capricorns are known for their discipline and strong work ethic. They are willing to put in the time and effort required to achieve their goals and often excel in their careers.

2. **Ambitious and Goal-Oriented**: Capricorn individuals are highly ambitious and set high standards for themselves. They are driven by a desire for success and recognition, and they work diligently to reach their objectives.

3. **Practical and Realistic**: Capricorns have a practical approach to life and are skilled at making realistic plans and decisions. They are resourceful and know how to use their strengths and resources to their advantage.

4. **Responsible and Reliable**: Capricorns take their responsibilities seriously and are known for their reliability. They are often seen as the pillars of their families and communities, providing support and guidance to others.

5. **Reserved and Patient**: While Capricorns are capable and confident, they tend to be reserved and patient. They understand the value of patience and are willing to wait for the right opportunities to achieve their goals.

Cannabis Strains: Offering Relaxation without Diminishing Focus for Capricorn's Drive

Given their disciplined and ambitious nature, Capricorn benefits from cannabis strains that offer relaxation without diminishing focus. The following strains are recommended to cater to Capricorn's hard-working and goal-oriented personality:

1. **Harlequin**: This sativa-dominant strain is high in CBD, providing clear-headed effects and enhancing focus without significant psychoactive impact. Harlequin is perfect for Capricorns who want to relax while maintaining mental clarity and productivity.

2. **ACDC**: Another high-CBD strain, ACDC offers soothing effects that alleviate anxiety and stress without causing a significant high. This strain is ideal for Capricorns who need to unwind while staying focused on their tasks.

3. **Blue Dream**: This well-balanced hybrid strain offers a gentle, uplifting high that promotes relaxation and mental clarity. Blue Dream is perfect for Capricorns who want to enjoy a creative flow without feeling too overwhelmed.

4. **Jack Herer**: Known for its stimulating and clear-headed effects, Jack Herer is a sativa-dominant strain that enhances creativity and focus. It's ideal for Capricorns who need an extra boost to tackle complex projects or stay productive throughout the day.

5. **Sour Tsunami**: This hybrid strain is known for its high CBD content and balanced effects, providing relaxation and stress relief without compromising mental clarity. Sour Tsunami is a great choice for Capricorns who want to relax while staying sharp and focused.

Consumption Settings: Environments for Reflecting on Personal and Professional Goals

Capricorn thrives in environments that allow them to reflect on their personal and professional goals. When using cannabis, the following settings and activities are ideal for Capricorn:

1. **Home Office or Study**: Create a dedicated home office or study space that is organized and free from distractions. Use a strain like Harlequin or Jack Herer to enhance focus and productivity while working on your goals and plans.
2. **Nature Retreats**: Spending time in nature can help Capricorns recharge and gain clarity on their goals. Whether it's a mountain cabin or a serene lakeside spot, a strain like Blue Dream can enhance your connection to nature and provide a sense of relaxation and inspiration.
3. **Meditation and Reflection**: Set aside time for meditation and reflection in a quiet, peaceful environment. Use a strain like ACDC or Sour Tsunami to promote relaxation and mental clarity, allowing you to focus on your aspirations and long-term plans.
4. **Personal Development Workshops**: Attending workshops or seminars focused on personal and professional development can be highly beneficial for Capricorns. Use a strain like Jack Herer to stay alert and engaged during the sessions, enhancing your learning experience.
5. **Evening Relaxation**: After a long day of work, create a relaxing evening routine that allows you to unwind and reflect on your achievements and future goals. Use a strain like Blue Dream to

promote relaxation while maintaining a sense of mental clarity and focus.

By understanding the unique traits and preferences of Capricorn, "The Celestial Stoner" provides tailored cannabis recommendations and consumption settings that align with their disciplined and ambitious nature. This personalized approach ensures that Capricorns can fully embrace their drive for success while enjoying the benefits of cannabis, creating an experience that is both relaxing and productive.

Check out my Virtual dispensary for all your hemp needs: https://shift.store/sg1fan23477/retail

Chapter 11: Aquarius: The Visionary Rebel
Zodiac Traits: Exploring Aquarius' Innovative and Unconventional Traits

Aquarius, the eleventh sign of the zodiac, is ruled by Uranus, the planet of innovation, sudden change, and unconventional thinking. Those born under this sign (January 20 - February 18) are known for their progressive, independent, and visionary nature. Represented by the Water Bearer, Aquarius individuals are forward-thinking and often ahead of their time, constantly seeking to challenge the status quo and bring new ideas into the world. They are intellectual, idealistic, and deeply committed to humanitarian causes.

Key traits of Aquarius include:

1. **Innovative and Forward-Thinking**: Aquarians are natural innovators who thrive on exploring new ideas and technologies. They are always looking for ways to improve and revolutionize the world around them.

2. **Independent and Unconventional**: Aquarius individuals value their independence and often take an unconventional approach to life. They are not afraid to go against the grain and pursue their unique path.

3. **Humanitarian and Idealistic**: Aquarians are deeply concerned with the well-being of humanity and are driven by a desire to make the world a better place. They are often involved in social causes and advocacy.

4. **Intellectual and Analytical**: Aquarius is an air sign, and those born under it are highly intellectual and analytical. They enjoy engaging in thought-provoking discussions and exploring complex concepts.

5. **Detached and Aloof**: While Aquarians are friendly and sociable, they can also be emotionally detached and aloof. They value their personal space and may struggle with forming deep emotional connections.

Cannabis Strains: Creative and Unusual Strains that Spark Innovation for Aquarius

Given their innovative and unconventional nature, Aquarius benefits from cannabis strains that spark creativity and innovation. The following strains are recommended to cater to Aquarius' visionary and inventive personality:

1. **Durban Poison**: This pure sativa strain is known for its energizing and uplifting effects. Durban Poison enhances creativity and mental clarity, making it perfect for Aquarians who want to engage in innovative thinking and problem-solving.
2. **Amnesia Haze**: Known for its cerebral and euphoric effects, Amnesia Haze is a sativa-dominant strain that stimulates creativity and provides a sense of mental clarity. It's ideal for Aquarians who want to explore new ideas and technologies.
3. **Lemon Skunk**: This sativa-dominant strain offers a burst of energy and creativity, making it suitable for Aquarians who need inspiration for their innovative projects. Its unique citrus flavor adds to the overall stimulating experience.
4. **Blue Dream**: This well-balanced hybrid strain provides a gentle, uplifting high that promotes creativity and relaxation. Blue Dream is perfect for Aquarians who want to enjoy a creative flow without feeling too overwhelmed.
5. **Pineapple Express**: Known for its balanced effects, Pineapple Express provides an energizing and euphoric high that enhances creativity and mental clarity. It's a great choice for Aquarians who want to stay active and inspired while working on their visionary ideas.

Consumption Settings: Eclectic and Tech-Oriented Environments for Aquarius' Inventive Side

Aquarius thrives in eclectic and tech-oriented environments that stimulate their inventive side. When using cannabis, the following environments and activities are ideal for Aquarius:

1. **Tech Labs and Innovation Hubs**: Aquarians love being at the forefront of technology and innovation. Spending time in tech labs or innovation hubs allows them to explore new gadgets and technologies. Use a strain like Durban Poison to stay energized and focused while tinkering with new inventions.

2. **Creative Workshops and Hackathons**: Participating in creative workshops or hackathons provides Aquarians with the opportunity to collaborate with like-minded individuals and develop innovative solutions. A strain like Amnesia Haze can enhance creativity and mental clarity during these events.

3. **Art Studios and Makerspaces**: Engaging in activities at art studios or makerspaces allows Aquarians to express their creativity and explore new artistic techniques. Use a strain like Lemon Skunk to stay inspired and energized while working on creative projects.

4. **Futuristic Lounges and VR Experiences**: Visiting futuristic lounges or trying out virtual reality (VR) experiences can provide Aquarians with a unique and stimulating environment. A strain like Blue Dream can enhance the overall experience and promote a sense of wonder and creativity.

5. **Outdoor Stargazing and Astronomy**: Aquarians are fascinated by the cosmos and often enjoy activities related to astronomy and stargazing. Spending time outdoors with a telescope or at an observatory can be a deeply inspiring experience. Use a strain like Pineapple Express to enhance your connection to the universe and spark new ideas.

By understanding the unique traits and preferences of Aquarius, "The Celestial Stoner" provides tailored cannabis recommendations and consumption settings that align with their innovative and unconventional nature. This personalized approach ensures that Aquarians can fully embrace their visionary personality while enjoying the benefits of cannabis, creating an experience that is both creatively stimulating and intellectually fulfilling.

Check out my Virtual dispensary for all your hemp needs: https://shift.store/sg1fan23477/retail

Chapter 12: Pisces: The Dreamy Poet
Zodiac Traits: Describing Pisces' Imaginative and Empathetic Nature

Pisces, the twelfth sign of the zodiac, is ruled by Neptune, the planet of dreams, intuition, and spirituality. Those born under this sign (February 19 - March 20) are known for their imaginative, empathetic, and deeply emotional nature. Represented by the Fish, Pisces individuals are often seen as the dreamers and poets of the zodiac, with a natural ability to tap into the collective unconscious and express their inner world through art, music, and writing. They are compassionate, intuitive, and have a profound sense of empathy for others.

Key traits of Pisces include:

1. **Imaginative and Creative**: Pisceans possess a vivid imagination and a deep well of creativity. They are often drawn to artistic pursuits and have a natural talent for expressing their emotions and ideas through various forms of art.

2. **Empathetic and Compassionate**: Pisces individuals are highly empathetic and compassionate, often feeling the emotions of others as if they were their own. They are known for their kindness and willingness to help those in need.

3. **Intuitive and Spiritual**: Pisces have a strong intuition and a deep connection to the spiritual and mystical realms. They often rely on their gut feelings and are drawn to exploring spiritual practices and philosophies.

4. **Gentle and Patient**: Pisceans are gentle and patient, preferring to avoid conflict and create a peaceful environment. They are often

seen as peacemakers and are skilled at diffusing tension with their calming presence.

5. **Dreamy and Escapist**: While their dreamy nature is a source of creativity, it can also make Pisces prone to escapism. They may retreat into their fantasies or seek out distractions when faced with harsh realities.

Cannabis Strains: Enhancing Creativity and Providing Emotional Depth for Pisces

Given their imaginative and empathetic nature, Pisces benefits from cannabis strains that enhance creativity and provide emotional depth. The following strains are recommended to cater to Pisces' dreamy and artistic personality:

1. **Blue Dream**: This well-balanced hybrid strain offers a gentle, uplifting high that enhances creativity and relaxation. Blue Dream is perfect for Pisceans who want to dive into their creative projects while maintaining a sense of calm and tranquility.

2. **Purple Haze**: Known for its euphoric and dreamy effects, Purple Haze is a sativa-dominant strain that stimulates creativity and provides a sense of emotional depth. It's ideal for Pisces who want to explore their artistic side and tap into their imagination.

3. **Cherry Pie**: This hybrid strain provides a balanced mix of euphoria and relaxation, making it suitable for Pisceans who want to enhance their creativity and emotional expression. Cherry Pie's sweet, berry flavor adds to the overall sensory experience.

4. **Lamb's Bread**: Known for its uplifting and inspirational effects, Lamb's Bread is a sativa strain that promotes creativity and a positive mindset. It's perfect for Pisces who want to feel inspired and motivated while working on their artistic endeavors.

5. **Jillybean**: This hybrid strain offers a joyful and creative high, providing a boost of energy and inspiration. Jillybean is ideal for

Pisceans who want to stay engaged and focused on their creative projects while enjoying a pleasant and uplifting experience.

Consumption Settings: Peaceful, Artistic Settings for Pisces to Dream and Create

Pisces thrives in peaceful, artistic settings that allow them to dream and create. When using cannabis, the following environments and activities are ideal for Pisces:

1. **Art Studios and Creative Spaces**: Pisces individuals love to immerse themselves in artistic environments where they can express their creativity freely. Use a strain like Purple Haze or Jillybean to enhance your artistic expression and enjoy a deep, creative flow.
2. **Quiet Beaches or Lakesides**: Spending time by the water is deeply soothing for Pisceans. A peaceful beach or lakeside setting can provide the perfect backdrop for reflection and creativity. Use a strain like Blue Dream to enhance the sense of calm and inspiration.
3. **Poetry Readings and Open Mic Nights**: Participating in or attending poetry readings and open mic nights allows Pisces to connect with other creative souls and share their work. A strain like Lamb's Bread can provide the inspiration and confidence needed to perform and engage with others.
4. **Meditation and Yoga Studios**: Engaging in meditation or yoga helps Pisces connect with their inner selves and find peace. A strain like Cherry Pie can enhance relaxation and emotional depth, allowing for a more profound and introspective practice.
5. **Home Sanctuary**: Creating a peaceful and artistic sanctuary at home can provide Pisceans with a safe space to dream and create. Use a strain like Blue Dream or Purple Haze to enhance your creative process while enjoying the comfort and tranquility of your own space.

By understanding the unique traits and preferences of Pisces, "The Celestial Stoner" provides tailored cannabis recommendations and consumption settings that align with their imaginative and empathetic nature. This personalized approach ensures that Pisceans can fully embrace their dreamy and artistic personality while enjoying the benefits of cannabis, creating an experience that is both creatively enriching and emotionally fulfilling.

Check out my Virtual dispensary for all your hemp needs: https://shift.store/sg1fan23477/retail

Conclusion: Your Astrological Cannabis Journey
Summary: Recapitulating Insights for Each Zodiac Sign and Their Relationship with Cannabis

Throughout "The Celestial Stoner: A Guide to the Zodiac," we have explored the unique characteristics and preferences of each zodiac sign, providing tailored cannabis recommendations and consumption settings that align with their distinct personalities and needs. By understanding the relationship between astrology and cannabis, we can enhance our experiences and deepen our connection to ourselves and the universe. Let's briefly recapitulate the insights provided for each sign:

1. **Aries: The Pioneering Spirit**
     - Traits: Dynamic, assertive, energetic
     - Strains: Energizing and stimulating (e.g., Green Crack, Sour Diesel)
     - Settings: Social and adventurous activities (e.g., outdoor adventures, parties)

2. **Taurus: The Sensual Connoisseur**
     - Traits: Comfort-loving, sensory-oriented, patient
     - Strains: Calming and sensory-enhancing (e.g., Blue Dream, Granddaddy Purple)
     - Settings: Cozy and luxurious environments (e.g., home spa, gourmet dining)

3. **Gemini: The Social Butterfly**
     - Traits: Communicative, sociable, curious
     - Strains: Uplifting and mentally stimulating (e.g., Super Silver Haze, Pineapple Express)

  - ◦ Settings: Dynamic social gatherings (e.g., trivia nights, book clubs)

4. **Cancer: The Comfort Seeker**
   - ◦ Traits: Emotional, nurturing, home-oriented
   - ◦ Strains: Calming and stress-relieving (e.g., Harlequin, Northern Lights)
   - ◦ Settings: Cozy and intimate environments (e.g., home sanctuary, family gatherings)

5. **Leo: The Radiant Star**
   - ◦ Traits: Charismatic, creative, ambitious
   - ◦ Strains: Energizing and creativity-enhancing (e.g., Sour Diesel, Tangie)
   - ◦ Settings: Performance and social settings (e.g., parties, creative workshops)

6. **Virgo: The Methodical Analyst**
   - ◦ Traits: Detail-oriented, analytical, practical
   - ◦ Strains: Focus-enhancing and clear-headed (e.g., Harlequin, Cinex)
   - ◦ Settings: Organized and serene environments (e.g., home office, gardening)

7. **Libra: The Harmonious Partner**
   - ◦ Traits: Balanced, diplomatic, social
   - ◦ Strains: Socially enhancing and calming (e.g., Blue Dream, Strawberry Cough)
   - ◦ Settings: Social and balanced environments (e.g., dinner parties, yoga classes)

8. **Scorpio: The Intense Investigator**
   - ◦ Traits: Intense, passionate, mysterious
   - ◦ Strains: Deep and potent (e.g., Northern Lights, Granddaddy Purple)
   - ◦ Settings: Transformative and introspective environments (e.g., meditation, deep conversations)

9. **Sagittarius: The Adventurous Philosopher**

- ◦ Traits: Adventurous, philosophical, optimistic
- ◦ Strains: Mind-stimulating and uplifting (e.g., Jack Herer, Sour Diesel)
- ◦ Settings: Outdoor and exploratory activities (e.g., hiking, cultural events)

10. **Capricorn: The Ambitious Climber**
- ◦ Traits: Disciplined, ambitious, responsible
- ◦ Strains: Relaxing without diminishing focus (e.g., Harlequin, Blue Dream)
- ◦ Settings: Reflective and goal-oriented environments (e.g., home office, nature retreats)

11. **Aquarius: The Visionary Rebel**
- ◦ Traits: Innovative, unconventional, intellectual
- ◦ Strains: Creative and unusual (e.g., Durban Poison, Amnesia Haze)
- ◦ Settings: Eclectic and tech-oriented environments (e.g., innovation hubs, VR experiences)

12. **Pisces: The Dreamy Poet**
- ◦ Traits: Imaginative, empathetic, intuitive
- ◦ Strains: Creativity-enhancing and emotionally deep (e.g., Blue Dream, Purple Haze)
- ◦ Settings: Peaceful and artistic environments (e.g., art studios, quiet beaches)

Integration: Encouraging Readers to Integrate Insights into Their Personal Cannabis Experience

As you reflect on the insights provided for your sun sign, consider integrating these recommendations into your personal cannabis experience. By aligning your cannabis use with your astrological profile, you can enhance both your wellbeing and enjoyment. But don't stop at your sun sign—consider exploring your moon sign and other aspects of your astrological chart for a deeper alignment.

- **Sun Sign**: Represents your core identity and personality. Use this guide to tailor your cannabis experience to your sun sign's traits and preferences.
- **Moon Sign**: Represents your emotional self and inner needs. Understanding your moon sign can help you choose cannabis strains and settings that provide emotional comfort and balance.
- **Rising Sign**: Reflects your outward behavior and how others perceive you. Consider your rising sign when selecting cannabis experiences for social interactions and public settings.

By incorporating these additional aspects of your astrological profile, you can create a more holistic and personalized approach to your cannabis journey.

Continued Exploration: Urging Readers to Explore Further

The interplay between your astrological profile and your cannabis use is a rich and dynamic field for exploration. Here are some ways to continue your journey:

1. **Keep a Cannabis and Astrology Journal**: Document your experiences with different strains and settings, noting how they align with your astrological profile. This practice can help you fine-tune your approach and discover new insights.
2. **Experiment with Different Strains**: Don't be afraid to try new strains and see how they affect you. Each strain has unique properties, and finding the right ones for your astrological makeup can be a rewarding journey.
3. **Explore Astrological Events**: Pay attention to astrological events like moon phases, planetary transits, and eclipses. Adjust your cannabis use to align with these events, enhancing your connection to the cosmos.
4. **Join a Community**: Engage with others who share your interest in astrology and cannabis. Online forums, local meetups, and

social media groups can provide support, inspiration, and new ideas for your journey.

By taking a personalized approach to your cannabis use, informed by your astrological profile, you can enhance your overall wellbeing, creativity, and enjoyment. "The Celestial Stoner: A Guide to the Zodiac" has provided you with the tools and insights to begin this journey. Now it's up to you to explore, experiment, and discover the unique ways in which cannabis and astrology can enrich your life.

Happy stargazing.

Appendix A: Cannabis Strain Guide
Detailed Profiles
This section provides detailed profiles of each recommended cannabis strain, including their effects, potential medical uses, and growing tips. Understanding the nuances of each strain will help you make informed decisions and tailor your cannabis experience to your astrological profile.

1. Blue Dream

- **Effects**: Balanced high with a gentle, uplifting euphoria and relaxing body effects. Enhances creativity and relaxation.
- **Medical Uses**: Effective for managing stress, anxiety, depression, pain, and headaches.
- **Growing Tips**: Blue Dream thrives in a sunny, Mediterranean climate. It has a flowering time of about 9-10 weeks and can produce high yields both indoors and outdoors.

2. Granddaddy Purple

- **Effects**: Heavy relaxation and calming properties with a sense of euphoria. Known for its powerful body high.
- **Medical Uses**: Ideal for treating chronic pain, insomnia, stress, and muscle spasms.
- **Growing Tips**: Prefers a warm, dry climate. Flowering time is approximately 8-11 weeks, and it is known for producing dense, purple buds with a sweet, grape-like aroma.

3. Green Crack

- **Effects**: Invigorating and focused high with a burst of energy and mental clarity.
- **Medical Uses**: Useful for combating fatigue, depression, and stress. Enhances focus and concentration.
- **Growing Tips**: Green Crack grows well in both indoor and outdoor settings. It has a short flowering period of 7-9 weeks and produces high yields.

4. Harlequin

- **Effects**: Clear-headed effects with enhanced focus and reduced anxiety. High in CBD with minimal psychoactive effects.
- **Medical Uses**: Effective for pain relief, anxiety, inflammation, and muscle spasms.
- **Growing Tips**: Harlequin requires a warm climate and consistent light exposure. It has a flowering time of 8-9 weeks and produces moderate yields.

5. Jack Herer

- **Effects**: Stimulating and clear-headed high with enhanced creativity and mental clarity.
- **Medical Uses**: Helpful for treating stress, depression, fatigue, and headaches.
- **Growing Tips**: Jack Herer thrives in a warm, Mediterranean climate. It has a flowering time of 8-10 weeks and produces high yields.

6. Lamb's Bread

- **Effects**: Uplifting and inspirational high that promotes creativity and a positive mindset.

- **Medical Uses**: Effective for managing stress, depression, and anxiety.
- **Growing Tips**: Lamb's Bread prefers a warm, sunny environment. It has a flowering period of about 7-9 weeks and produces moderate yields.

7. Northern Lights

- **Effects**: Deep relaxation and tranquility with a strong body high. Promotes restful sleep.
- **Medical Uses**: Ideal for treating insomnia, pain, stress, and anxiety.
- **Growing Tips**: Northern Lights is a hardy strain that grows well indoors and outdoors. It has a short flowering time of 6-8 weeks and produces high yields.

8. OG Kush

- **Effects**: Strong and long-lasting effects with a powerful body high and mental clarity.
- **Medical Uses**: Effective for managing stress, pain, insomnia, and depression.
- **Growing Tips**: OG Kush prefers a warm, sunny climate. It has a flowering time of 8-9 weeks and produces moderate to high yields.

9. Pineapple Express

- **Effects**: Energizing and euphoric high with enhanced creativity and mental clarity.
- **Medical Uses**: Useful for treating depression, anxiety, fatigue, and mild pain.

- **Growing Tips**: Pineapple Express thrives in a warm, tropical climate. It has a flowering time of 7-9 weeks and produces high yields.

10. Purple Haze

- **Effects**: Euphoric and dreamy effects with enhanced creativity and mental clarity.
- **Medical Uses**: Effective for managing stress, depression, and chronic pain.
- **Growing Tips**: Purple Haze prefers a warm, sunny environment. It has a flowering time of 9-10 weeks and produces moderate yields.

11. Sour Diesel

- **Effects**: Energizing and uplifting high with enhanced mental stimulation and focus.
- **Medical Uses**: Useful for treating stress, depression, fatigue, and pain.
- **Growing Tips**: Sour Diesel thrives in a warm, Mediterranean climate. It has a flowering time of 9-10 weeks and produces high yields.

12. Super Silver Haze

- **Effects**: Balanced high with stimulating and euphoric effects. Enhances creativity and mental clarity.
- **Medical Uses**: Effective for managing stress, depression, fatigue, and migraines.
- **Growing Tips**: Super Silver Haze prefers a warm, humid climate. It has a flowering time of 9-11 weeks and produces high yields.

13. Strawberry Cough

- **Effects**: Uplifting and mentally stimulating high with a sense of euphoria and relaxation.
- **Medical Uses**: Useful for treating stress, depression, fatigue, and anxiety.
- **Growing Tips**: Strawberry Cough grows well indoors and in warm climates. It has a flowering time of 9-10 weeks and produces moderate yields.

14. White Widow

- **Effects**: Balanced high with a mix of euphoria and relaxation. Enhances creativity and mental clarity.
- **Medical Uses**: Effective for managing stress, depression, pain, and insomnia.
- **Growing Tips**: White Widow thrives in a warm, sunny environment. It has a flowering time of 8-9 weeks and produces high yields.

15. ACDC

- **Effects**: Soothing effects with minimal psychoactive impact. High in CBD, providing relaxation and stress relief.
- **Medical Uses**: Ideal for treating pain, anxiety, inflammation, and muscle spasms.
- **Growing Tips**: ACDC requires a warm climate and consistent light exposure. It has a flowering time of 9-10 weeks and produces moderate yields.

16. Amnesia Haze

- **Effects**: Cerebral and euphoric effects with enhanced creativity and mental clarity.
- **Medical Uses**: Useful for treating stress, depression, fatigue, and anxiety.
- **Growing Tips**: Amnesia Haze thrives in a warm, Mediterranean climate. It has a longer flowering time of 10-12 weeks but produces high yields.

17. Cherry Pie

- **Effects**: Balanced mix of euphoria and relaxation with enhanced creativity and emotional expression.
- **Medical Uses**: Effective for managing stress, depression, anxiety, and pain.
- **Growing Tips**: Cherry Pie prefers a warm, sunny environment. It has a flowering time of 8-9 weeks and produces moderate to high yields.

18. Jillybean

- **Effects**: Joyful and creative high with a boost of energy and inspiration.
- **Medical Uses**: Useful for treating stress, depression, fatigue, and mild pain.
- **Growing Tips**: Jillybean thrives in a warm, sunny climate. It has a flowering time of 8-9 weeks and produces moderate yields.

Pairing Strains with Astrological Events

Astrological events such as retrogrades, eclipses, and planetary alignments can significantly influence our mood, energy, and overall well-being. Selecting the right cannabis strain during these times can help you navigate these cosmic shifts with greater ease and alignment. Here are some guidelines for pairing strains with specific astrological events:

1. Retrogrades

- **Mercury Retrograde**: Known for causing communication mishaps and technical glitches, Mercury retrograde can be a stressful time. Choose calming and clear-headed strains like Harlequin or ACDC to stay grounded and focused.
- **Venus Retrograde**: This period can bring up relationship issues and self-reflection. Use strains like Blue Dream or Cherry Pie to enhance emotional balance and promote positive introspection.
- **Mars Retrograde**: Mars retrograde can lead to frustration and low energy. Opt for energizing strains like Green Crack or Sour Diesel to boost motivation and combat lethargy.

2. Eclipses

- **Solar Eclipses**: These events signify new beginnings and dramatic shifts. Enhance your creativity and open-mindedness with strains like Amnesia Haze or Jack Herer to embrace new opportunities.
- **Lunar Eclipses**: Lunar eclipses often bring emotional revelations and endings. Use calming and introspective strains like Northern Lights or Granddaddy Purple to navigate emotional intensity and release old patterns.

3. Planetary Alignments

- **Conjunctions**: When planets align closely, their combined energy can be intense. Balance this intensity with strains like White Widow or Pineapple Express to maintain equilibrium and harness the power of the alignment.
- **Oppositions**: Oppositions create tension and highlight areas of conflict. Choose soothing strains like Blue Dream or Lamb's Bread to ease tension and promote harmony.

- **Trines:** These harmonious alignments bring ease and flow. Enhance the positive energy with uplifting strains like Lemon Skunk or Strawberry Cough to fully enjoy the benefits of the trine.

By understanding the unique properties of each cannabis strain and their potential effects during astrological events, you can create a personalized approach that enhances both your wellbeing and enjoyment. Embrace the interplay between your astrological profile and your cannabis use, and let the stars guide your journey to greater harmony and fulfillment.

Appendix B: Astrology for Beginners
Basic Concepts: A Primer on the Basics of Astrology

Astrology is the study of the movements and relative positions of celestial bodies interpreted as having an influence on human affairs and the natural world. This ancient practice has been used for thousands of years to gain insights into personality, predict events, and guide decisions. Understanding the basics of astrology can enhance your appreciation of how it interacts with your cannabis experience. Here, we cover fundamental concepts and how to interpret a natal chart.

1. The Zodiac Signs

The zodiac is divided into twelve signs, each associated with specific traits and ruled by different planets. The signs are:

1. **Aries (March 21 - April 19)**: Dynamic, assertive, energetic.
2. **Taurus (April 20 - May 20)**: Comfort-loving, sensory-oriented, patient.
3. **Gemini (May 21 - June 20)**: Communicative, sociable, curious.
4. **Cancer (June 21 - July 22)**: Emotional, nurturing, home-oriented.
5. **Leo (July 23 - August 22)**: Charismatic, creative, ambitious.
6. **Virgo (August 23 - September 22)**: Detail-oriented, analytical, practical.
7. **Libra (September 23 - October 22)**: Balanced, diplomatic, social.
8. **Scorpio (October 23 - November 21)**: Intense, passionate, mysterious.
9. **Sagittarius (November 22 - December 21)**: Adventurous, philosophical, optimistic.
10. **Capricorn (December 22 - January 19)**: Disciplined, ambitious, responsible.

11. **Aquarius (January 20 - February 18)**: Innovative, unconventional, intellectual.
12. **Pisces (February 19 - March 20)**: Imaginative, empathetic, intuitive.

2. The Planets

In astrology, each planet represents different aspects of life and personality:

1. **Sun**: Core identity and ego.
2. **Moon**: Emotions and inner self.
3. **Mercury**: Communication and intellect.
4. **Venus**: Love and relationships.
5. **Mars**: Action and desire.
6. **Jupiter**: Expansion and growth.
7. **Saturn**: Discipline and responsibility.
8. **Uranus**: Innovation and change.
9. **Neptune**: Dreams and intuition.
10. **Pluto**: Transformation and power.

3. Houses

The natal chart is divided into twelve houses, each representing different areas of life:

1. **1st House**: Self and appearance.
2. **2nd House**: Finances and values.
3. **3rd House**: Communication and siblings.
4. **4th House**: Home and family.
5. **5th House**: Creativity and romance.
6. **6th House**: Health and work.
7. **7th House**: Partnerships and marriage.
8. **8th House**: Transformation and shared resources.
9. **9th House**: Travel and higher education.

10. **10th House**: Career and public life.
11. **11th House**: Friends and social causes.
12. **12th House**: Subconscious and spirituality.

4. Aspects

Aspects are the angles between planets in the natal chart, influencing how they interact:

1. **Conjunction (0°)**: Planets are aligned, intensifying their energies.
2. **Sextile (60°)**: Positive, harmonious interaction.
3. **Square (90°)**: Tension and challenges.
4. **Trine (120°)**: Easy flow and support.
5. **Opposition (180°)**: Polarity and balance.

Interpreting a Natal Chart

A natal chart, or birth chart, is a snapshot of the sky at the moment of your birth. To interpret it:

1. **Gather Your Birth Information**: You need your birth date, time, and location.
2. **Create Your Natal Chart**: Use an online astrology calculator or consult an astrologer.
3. **Identify Your Sun, Moon, and Rising Signs**: These are the most influential placements.
   - **Sun Sign**: Core personality.
   - **Moon Sign**: Emotional nature.
   - **Rising Sign**: Outward behavior and first impressions.
4. **Examine the Planets and Houses**: Note the sign and house of each planet to understand different life areas.
5. **Analyze Aspects**: Look at the relationships between planets for deeper insights.

Understanding Personal Astrology: Tips for Making Informed Decisions

Astrology can be a powerful tool for self-awareness and decision-making. Here's how you can use it to enhance your life and cannabis experience:

1. **Know Your Sun and Moon Signs**: Your sun sign reflects your core identity, while your moon sign reveals your emotional needs. Consider both when choosing cannabis strains and settings to balance your experience.
   - **Sun Sign**: Align strains and activities with your core traits (e.g., energizing strains for Aries' dynamism).
   - **Moon Sign**: Choose strains that address emotional needs (e.g., calming strains for a Cancer moon).
2. **Use Astrology for Timing**: Align your cannabis use with astrological events to maximize benefits.
   - **New Moon**: New beginnings and intentions. Try uplifting strains to boost creativity and inspiration.
   - **Full Moon**: Reflection and release. Use calming strains to facilitate emotional processing.
   - **Mercury Retrograde**: Communication challenges. Opt for clear-headed strains to stay grounded and focused.
3. **Understand Your Houses**: Each house in your chart affects different life areas. Use this knowledge to address specific needs with cannabis.
   - **6th House (Health)**: Focus on strains that promote physical well-being and relaxation.
   - **9th House (Learning and Travel)**: Choose stimulating strains for intellectual pursuits and exploration.
4. **Analyze Planetary Transits**: Current planetary movements impact your natal chart, influencing mood and behavior.

- ○ **Saturn Return**: A time of significant life changes (around age 29 and 58). Use introspective strains to navigate this transformative period.
- ○ **Jupiter Transits**: Opportunities for growth. Energizing strains can help you seize new opportunities.

5. **Track Your Experiences**: Keep a journal of your cannabis use and astrological influences. Note how different strains and astrological events affect your mood, creativity, and overall well-being. This can help you refine your approach and make more informed choices.

6. **Explore Complementary Practices**: Combine astrology with other holistic practices for a well-rounded approach.
- ○ **Meditation**: Use calming strains and meditate during significant astrological events for deeper insights.
- ○ **Yoga**: Align your practice with lunar phases and use strains that enhance focus and relaxation.

By integrating these astrological insights into your cannabis experience, you can create a more personalized and fulfilling journey. Embrace the wisdom of the stars to enhance your well-being, creativity, and enjoyment. Whether you're a seasoned stargazer or new to astrology, this guide provides the tools you need to explore the interplay between your astrological profile and cannabis use.

Message from the Author:

I hope you enjoyed this book, I love astrology and knew there was not a book such as this out on the shelf. I love metaphysical items as well. Please check out my other books:

-Life of Government Benefits

-My life of Hell

-My life with Hydrocephalus

-Red Sky

-World Domination:Woman's rule

-World Domination:Woman's Rule 2: The War

-Life and Banishment of Apophis: book 1

-The Kidney Friendly Diet

-The Ultimate Hemp Cookbook

-Creating a Dispensary(legally)

-Cleanliness throughout life: the importance of showering from childhood to adulthood.

-Strong Roots: The Risks of Overcoddling children

-Hemp Horoscopes: Cosmic Insights and Earthly Healing

- Celestial Hemp Navigating the Zodiac: Through the Green Cosmos

-Astrological Hemp: Aligning The Stars with Earth's Ancient Herb

-The Astrological Guide to Hemp: Stars, Signs, and Sacred Leaves

-Green Growth: Innovative Marketing Strategies for your Hemp Products and Dispensary

-Cosmic Cannabis

-Astrological Munchies

-Henry The Hemp

-Zodiacal Roots: The Astrological Soul Of Hemp

- **Green Constellations: Intersection of Hemp and Zodiac**

-Hemp in The Houses: An astrological Adventure Through The Cannabis Galaxy

-Galactic Ganja Guide

Heavenly Hemp

Zodiac Leaves

Doctor Who Astrology

Cannastrology

Stellar Satvias and Cosmic Indicas

Celestial Cannabis: A Zodiac Journey

AstroHerbology: The Sky and The Soil: Volume 1

AstroHerbology:Celestial Cannabis:Volume 2

Cosmic Cannabis Cultivation

The Starry Guide to Herbal Harmony: Volume 1

The Starry Guide to Herbal Harmony: Cannabis Universe: Volume 2

Yugioh Astrology: Astrological Guide to Deck, Duels and more

Nightmare Mansion: Echoes of The Abyss

Nightmare Mansion 2: Legacy of Shadows

Nightmare Mansion 3: Shadows of the Forgotten

Nightmare Mansion 4: Echoes of the Damned

The Life and Banishment of Apophis: Book 2

Nightmare Mansion: Halls of Despair

Healing with Herb: Cannabis and Hydrocephalus

Planetary Pot: Aligning with Astrological Herbs: Volume 1

Fast Track to Freedom: 30 Days to Financial Independence Using AI, Assets, and Agile Hustles

Cosmic Hemp Pathways

How to Become Financially Free in 30 Days: 10,000 Paths to Prosperity

Zodiacal Herbage: Astrological Insights: Volume 1

Nightmare Mansion: Whispers in the Walls

The Daleks Invade Atlantis

Henry the hemp and Hydrocephalus

10X The Kidney Friendly Diet

Cannabis Universe: Adult coloring book

Hemp Astrology: The Healing Power of the Stars

Zodiacal Herbage: Astrological Insights: Cannabis Universe: Volume 2

Planetary Pot: Aligning with Astrological Herbs: Cannabis Universes: Volume 2

Doctor Who Meets the Replicators and SG-1: The Ultimate Battle for Survival

Nightmare Mansion: Curse of the Blood Moon

Check out my Virtual dispensary for all your hemp needs: https://shift.store/sg1fan23477/retail

If you want solar for your home go here: 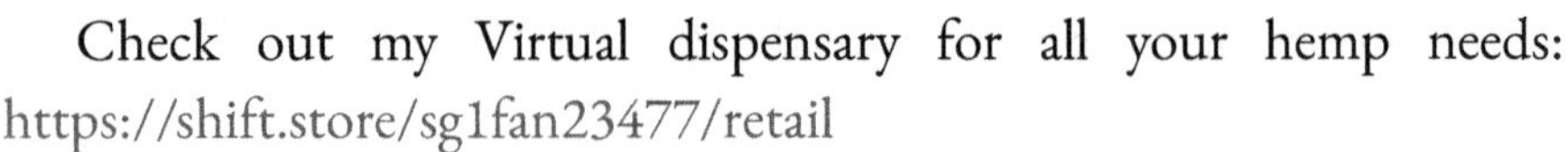https://www.harborsolar.live/apophisenterprises/

Get Some Tarot cards: https://www.makeplayingcards.com/sell/apophis-occult-shop

Get some shirts: https://www.bonfire.com/store/apophis-shirt-emporium/

Instagrams:
@apophis_enterprises,
@hempkingdom2024,
@apophisbookemporium,
@apophisfashion,
@apophisscardshop

Twitter: @apophisenterpr1,

Tiktok:@apophisenterprise

Youtube: @sg1fan23477

Podcast: ApophisChat Zone: https://open.spotify.com/show/5zXbrCLEV2xzCp8ybrfHsk?si=fb4d4fdbdce44dec

Newsletter: https://apophiss-newsletter-27c897.beehiiv.com/